BLACK LIVES MATTER

BY DUCHESS HARRIS, JD, PHD

Core Library

An Imprint of Abdo Publishing
abdopublishing.com

Cover image: Black Lives Matter supporters chant at a
Texas rally.

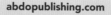

abdopublishing.com

Published by Abdo Publishing, a division of ABDO, PO Box 398166, Minneapolis, Minnesota 55439. Copyright © 2018 by Abdo Consulting Group, Inc. International copyrights reserved in all countries. No part of this book may be reproduced in any form without written permission from the publisher. Core Library™ is a trademark and logo of Abdo Publishing.

Printed in the United States of America, North Mankato, Minnesota
092017
012018

THIS BOOK CONTAINS
RECYCLED MATERIALS

Cover Photo: Joel Martinez/The Monitor/AP Images
Interior Photos: Joel Martinez/The Monitor/AP Images, 1; Huy Mach/St. Louis Post-Dispatch/AP Images, 4–5, 7; Laurence Heyworth/Montagu Images/Alamy, 12–13; William P. Straeter/AP Images, 17; Red Line Editorial, 18, 36; Tampa Bay Times/ZumaPress/Newscom, 20–21; Richard Ulreich/ZumaPress/Newscom, 26–27; Aaron Lavinsky/Star Tribune/AP Images, 30; Ron Egozi/Photoshot/Newscom, 32–33; David J. Phillip/AP Images, 39

Editor: Marie Pearson
Imprint Designer: Maggie Villaume
Series Design Direction: Claire Mathiowetz
Contributor: Valerie Bodden

Publisher's Cataloging-in-Publication Data

Names: Harris, Duchess, author.
Title: Black lives matter / by Duchess Harris.
Description: Minneapolis, Minnesota : Abdo Publishing, 2018. | Series: Protest movements | Includes online resources and index.
Identifiers: LCCN 2017947126 | ISBN 9781532113949 (lib.bdg.) | ISBN 9781532152825 (ebook)
Subjects: LCSH: Black lives matter movement--Juvenile literature. | Racial profiling in law enforcement--United States--Juvenile literature. | African Americans--Social conditions--Juvenile literature. | Protest movements--Juvenile literature.
Classification: DDC 305.89607309--dc23
LC record available at https://lccn.loc.gov/2017947126

CONTENTS

HANDS UP, DON'T SHOOT

It was just after noon on Saturday, August 9, 2014. Gunshots echoed through the Canfield Green apartment complex. The complex was in Ferguson, outside of Saint Louis, Missouri. Residents rushed to their windows and doors. Some poured into the streets. There, they found two white police officers. The officers stood near the body of Michael Brown, an 18-year-old African-American man. Brown had been shot by Darren Wilson, one of the officers.

Police kept onlookers from approaching the shooting site.

A crowd quickly gathered at the site. Many pulled out their phones to take photos and videos. As time passed, the crowd grew to hundreds of people. Many became restless. They wanted to know why Brown had been shot. They wondered why his body remained on the ground hours later. More police officers arrived. Some came in armored vehicles. Others led police dogs. Many wore full riot gear.

After four and a half hours, police finished their on-scene investigation. They removed Brown's body from the site. There is no police standard for how long a body should remain on the ground after a shooting. But many people in the crowd were angry that Brown's body had remained in the open so long. They felt it took away Brown's dignity.

Brown's mother approached the spot where the body had been. The crowd followed. Some laid flowers and candles on the ground. The crowd prayed and sang together.

Brown's mother scattered rose petals on the spot where he was killed.

As night fell, the crowds remained. They raised their hands into the air. Many shouted, "Hands up, don't shoot!" They believed these to be Brown's last words, though a later report said that Brown likely didn't have his hands up when he was shot. That night, someone set a dumpster on fire.

JUSTICE DEPARTMENT REPORT

After Michael Brown's death, the US Justice Department investigated the Ferguson Police Department. It found that Ferguson's mostly white police officers purposely discriminated against black residents. Ferguson officers targeted black people for minor violations. Those who failed to pay even small fines often faced arrest. Officers illegally searched black people. In some cases, they released police dogs on unarmed children. The findings led Ferguson police chief Thomas Jackson to quit.

GOING VIRAL

The next day, many people in the crowd posted updates to Facebook and Twitter. Videos showed Brown's parents grieving for their son. Photos of police in riot gear hit the Internet in real time. Soon local TV crews arrived as well.

Thousands of people began protesting in Ferguson's streets. As day became night, peaceful protests turned violent. Rioters broke car windows, smashed storefronts, and burned down a gas station. Police responded by releasing tear gas. They shot rubber bullets into the crowd. They hit both peaceful and violent protesters. This continued throughout the week. Some rioters threw rocks and bricks at officers. The officers responded with tear gas and pepper spray. They arrested more than 150 people. Most of the arrests were for refusing to leave the protests.

Stories of the chaos hit social media. National media outlets also covered

PERSPECTIVES
YOUNG ACTIVIST

Black high school student Clifton Kinnie lived only minutes from Ferguson. He saw an Instagram post about the riots there. He had to see them for himself. During a peaceful protest, Kinnie was tear gassed by police. He was angry when a teacher later complained about the protesters. The teacher said nothing about the police response. Kinnie took action. He formed Our Destiny STL to involve young people in activism. Our Destiny STL organized marches. The group also held voter registration drives. In 2016 Kinnie received the Ambassador Andrew Young Distinguished Leader Award for his activism. Young was a leader in the civil rights movement.

the protests. Events in Ferguson became one of the nation's top news stories.

BLACK LIVES MATTER

People posted about Ferguson on social media. Many added the hashtag #BlackLivesMatter to their posts. The hashtag had been created in 2013. It had first been used after the shooting of Trayvon Martin, a young black man from Florida. The hashtag hadn't been used much during the two years since Martin's death. But it now sprang up everywhere.

Soon protesters made a hashtag into a social movement. By 2017 the Black Lives Matter movement had produced a new generation of black activists. They protested police brutality. They wanted to end discrimination in the criminal justice system. They demanded better housing. Most of all, they wanted equality in the United States and around the world.

STRAIGHT TO THE
SOURCE

Kareem "Tef Poe" Jackson is a rapper from Saint Louis. After Brown's shooting, he published a letter to President Barack Obama:

> *When an assault rifle is aimed at your face over nothing more than a refusal to move, you don't feel like the American experience is one that includes you. When the president your generation selected does not condemn these attacks, you suddenly begin to believe that this system is a fraudulent hoax—and the joke is on you. Racism is very much alive in America, but as a [black] president . . . you seem to address it very bashfully. . . . Right now we are being treated like enemies of the state while the racist police force continues to arm itself and occupy our communities.*

> Source: Tef Poe. "Dear Mr. President: A Letter from Tef Poe." *The Riverfront Times.* The Riverfront Times, December 1, 2014. Web. Accessed July 13, 2017.

Back It Up

The author of this passage is using evidence to support a point. Write a paragraph describing the point the author is making. Then write down two or three pieces of evidence the author uses to make the point.

A LONG HISTORY

Racial tension in the United States dates back to the arrival of the first slaves from Africa in 1619. Enslaved Africans did not have the same rights as white people. Instead they were bought and sold as property. They were forced to work on farms and plantations. Many faced beatings.

In the early 1800s, reformers started the abolition, or anti-slavery, movement. Many reformers were African Americans. The conflict over slavery became a major issue during the American Civil War (1861–1865). When the war ended, slavery was outlawed.

An artist depicts a slave auction, where slaveholders bought and sold enslaved Africans, sometimes tearing apart families.

CIVIL RIGHTS AND BLACK POWER

But the end of slavery did not end racial tension. In some places, black men were lynched by large mobs. Across the South, segregation kept black and white people separate. African-American children had to attend their own schools. Movie theaters, restaurants, and even restrooms were divided by race.

By the 1950s, these policies had sparked the civil rights movement. Young people became involved in the movement. In 1961 many participated in Freedom Rides. On these bus trips, groups of black and white people traveled to Southern cities. They refused to follow local segregation laws. In some cities, Freedom

ABOLITIONISTS

Some abolitionists, such as Frederick Douglass, had escaped slavery. Their stories encouraged others to join the cause. Abolitionists gave lectures and had petition drives. Some used force to block the return of escaped slaves to their owners.

Riders were arrested. In others, they faced attacks from angry mobs.

In 1963 civil rights leader Martin Luther King Jr. organized the Children's Crusade in Birmingham, Alabama. Police met child and teenage protesters with dogs and fire hoses. Police arrested many children. The clash was caught by TV cameras. It was broadcast to homes across the country. Many were angry. The next year, Congress passed the

PERSPECTIVES
LITTLE ROCK NINE

In 1954 the Supreme Court ruled school segregation unconstitutional. All schools were ordered to accept African-American students. But the process was slow. On September 4, 1957, nine African-American students tried to enter Central High School in Little Rock, Arkansas. White mobs and National Guard troops blocked their way. The students finally entered the school two weeks later. Federal troops protected them. That spring, Ernest Green became the first African American to graduate from the school. He and the other students became known as the Little Rock Nine.

Civil Rights Act. This act made segregation and racial discrimination illegal.

The new law was a major victory. But many felt it did not go far enough. In many places, black people continued to suffer from poverty and poor housing. Young black men were often the targets of police brutality. In the late 1960s, the Black Power movement emerged. Leaders of the movement sought liberation, or freedom, from oppression. They were willing to use any means necessary, including violence. Some Black Power activists formed a group known as the Black Panthers. The Black Panthers patrolled streets to protect black people from police brutality. They often took part in violent clashes with police officers. But they also provided social programs, such as breakfast for children. In 1969 Chicago Black Panther leader Fred Hampton was shot and killed by police.

The Black Panthers gave free breakfast to schoolchildren whose families didn't have enough money to feed them three meals a day.

RACE REBELLION

Race relations seemed to improve in the 1970s and 1980s. Black people found more opportunities in colleges and the workplaces. But in March 1991, four white police officers in Los Angeles, California, beat black motorist Rodney King after a high-speed chase. In April 1992, the officers were found not guilty. For the

AFRICAN AMERICANS IN
CONGRESS

African-American men were given the right to vote in 1870. That same year, the first black people were elected to the US Congress. There are 100 seats in the Senate and 435 in the House of Representatives. What do you notice about the number of black people in Congress over time? What does this suggest about race relations in the United States?

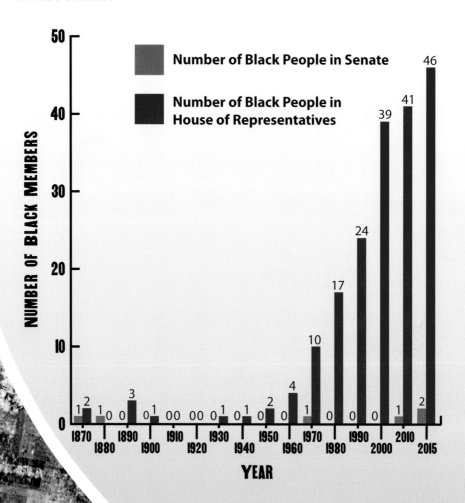

next five days, riots broke out across Los Angeles. More than 50 people died in the riots, and 2,000 were injured.

BEYOND RACE

By the early 2000s, many people found hope in the rising number of black elected officials. In 2007, 43 African Americans served in the US Congress. In 2009, Barack Obama became the nation's first black president. Obama's election led many people to hope racial discrimination had come to an end.

FURTHER EVIDENCE

Chapter Two discusses the history of race relations in the United States. What was one of the main points of this chapter? What key evidence supports this point? Read the article at the website below. Does the information on the website support the main point of the chapter? Does it offer new evidence?

PBS AFRICANS IN AMERICA: ABOLITIONISM
abdocorelibrary.com/black-lives-matter

GROWING AWARENESS

Despite the election of an African-American president in 2008, black people continued to face inequalities. Many cities were still unofficially segregated into black and white communities. Black communities often faced poverty and poor housing. Many could not get good health care. Public schools in black communities often weren't given enough money.

In many black communities, the police force was almost entirely white. This often

Parents, including Shavon Flournoy, were angered when the principal of Campbell Park Elementary School in Florida suggested that all white students should be in the same class.

led to tension between community members and police officers. This tension at times erupted into violence and death. Police shootings of young, unarmed black men made headlines in many cities. Among the victims was 22-year-old Oscar Grant. In 2009 Grant was shot by an officer in Oakland, California. Grant was lying face down on the ground when he was shot. Bystanders recorded the shooting and posted it online. The shooting sparked violent protests. But the protests died down after a few weeks.

TRAYVON MARTIN

On February 26, 2012, 17-year-old Trayvon Martin was walking down the street in Sanford, Florida. He had his hood up against the rain. Martin was confronted by George Zimmerman, a white neighborhood watch volunteer. Zimmerman later said Martin punched him and knocked him down. He said he pulled his gun in self-defense. He shot Martin in the chest, killing him. There were no witnesses. Police could find no evidence to disprove Zimmerman's claim. They let him go.

Reports of Martin's death spread on TV and social media. Thousands of people held rallies to protest the killing. Two million people signed online petitions demanding Zimmerman's arrest. Six weeks later, Zimmerman was arrested. He was charged with second-degree murder. On July 13, 2013, Zimmerman was acquitted. Many people thought violence would break out at the verdict. Instead, peaceful protesters gathered to hold rallies and vigils, or quiet night gatherings. Many wore hoodies to show their support for Martin.

ORGANIZING FOR ACTION

George Zimmerman's acquittal led to the formation of several new activist groups. The Dream Defenders called for nonviolent action to end police brutality. The organization held a 31-day sit-in at the Florida governor's office. The Million Hoodies Movement for Justice was also formed. It sought to change media portrayals of black men. Both organizations began as local groups in Miami, Florida. Million Hoodies later expanded to become a national organization.

A JOURNALIST ON THE SCENE

Brittany Noble-Jones was a TV reporter in Saint Louis. She was one of only a few black reporters for her station. On August 9, 2014, Noble-Jones saw a social media post about Michael Brown's death. She e-mailed her boss to ask if anyone from the station was on the scene. No one was. She arrived in time to capture emotional footage of Brown's mother. Over the following hours, Noble-Jones broadcast live reports from the protests. She later said this police shooting felt different from others she had covered. The response of the community and the police seemed larger.

A NEW HASHTAG

Oakland, California, resident Alicia Garza heard about Zimmerman's acquittal. She posted on Facebook her disgust at the verdict. The 31-year-old black woman wrote that the nation seemed to think black lives didn't matter. But, she said, black lives do matter. Garza's friends and fellow activists Patrisse Cullors and Opal Tometi liked the phrase. The three women began using it as a hashtag. #BlackLivesMatter was born. By the end of the year, the hashtag had been used 5,000 times.

Black deaths continued the next year. Details of Brown's shooting raced across social media in August 2014. As a result, #BlackLivesMatter took on a new life. An average of 59,000 tweets a day used the hashtag. But Black Lives Matter was about to move beyond social media. It would soon become a movement for social justice.

EXPLORE ONLINE

Chapter Three talks about the George Zimmerman trial. The article at the website below goes into more depth on this topic. How does the article add to your understanding of those protesting the verdict?

ZIMMERMAN TRIAL

abdocorelibrary.com/black-lives-matter

CHAPTER
FOUR

ON THE GROUND

Weeks of protests in Ferguson followed Brown's death. After the first week, most protests remained calm. At the end of August, hundreds of people took part in Freedom Rides. The rides were modeled on those of the civil rights movement. They brought busloads of people from many cities around the country to Ferguson to protest.

MORE DEATHS

As protests continued, reports of black men shot by police officers continued to rock the Saint Louis area. On October 13, tens

People of all ages came to Ferguson to protest Brown's shooting.

of thousands of people gathered in Ferguson for Ferguson October. This event included protests and acts of civil disobedience. Dozens of clergy gathered on the grounds of the Ferguson police department. Many were arrested. Other protesters blocked downtown roads. They played hopscotch, jump rope, and other children's games. They wanted to show that officials were treating the loss of black lives as a game.

THE MOVEMENT SPREADS

Protests spread to cities across the nation.

Many demonstrators took up the chant "black lives matter." Garza, Cullors, and Tometi formed the Black Lives Matter network. This national organization is made up of chapters in several US cities. The chapters work to fight racism and police violence. Many chapters also expanded their movement to include education, health care, and other areas of inequality. Other new civil rights groups formed both locally and nationally. These organizations were seen by the media and the public as part of the larger Black Lives Matter movement.

Many of the new organizations used similar tactics. Activists gathered at shopping malls to disrupt shoppers. They blocked highways and shut down train service in some cities. Some held die-ins, lying on the ground as if dead. The goal of these types of protests was to make people uncomfortable. Protesters wanted people to think about the frustration felt by black people every day. Activists used social media to quickly organize actions and spread footage of events.

Demonstrators filled the Mall of America in 2014 and chanted, "Black lives matter."

Not all activists agreed with such disruptive tactics. Some believed education would bring better results. They organized booths at public events. They talked with people and gave out information.

MORE REASONS FOR PROTEST

No matter their tactics, activists took notice of each new police shooting. On November 22, 2014, 12-year-old Tamir Rice was playing with a toy gun in a Cleveland, Ohio, park. He was shot by officers who thought the gun was real. Rice's death sparked a new round of protests. Unlike in Ferguson, police in Cleveland worked with demonstrators. The protests remained peaceful.

Two days after Rice's death, officials in Ferguson said Darren Wilson would not be charged with a crime for shooting Brown. Protests in Ferguson again turned violent. Just more than a week later, New York City officials decided not to charge the officer responsible for Eric Garner's death. Garner had died when a police officer put him in a choke hold. Large-scale demonstrations shut down bridges and tunnels across the city.

BACK THE BADGE

Some people worried that good police officers faced hatred and anger as a result of the Black Lives Matter movement. To show support for officers, some people used the #BlueLivesMatter hashtag, but others felt this name took away from important issues Black Lives Matter raised. People displayed "We Back the Badge" yard signs. Some cities held rallies for police officers.

CHAPTER FIVE

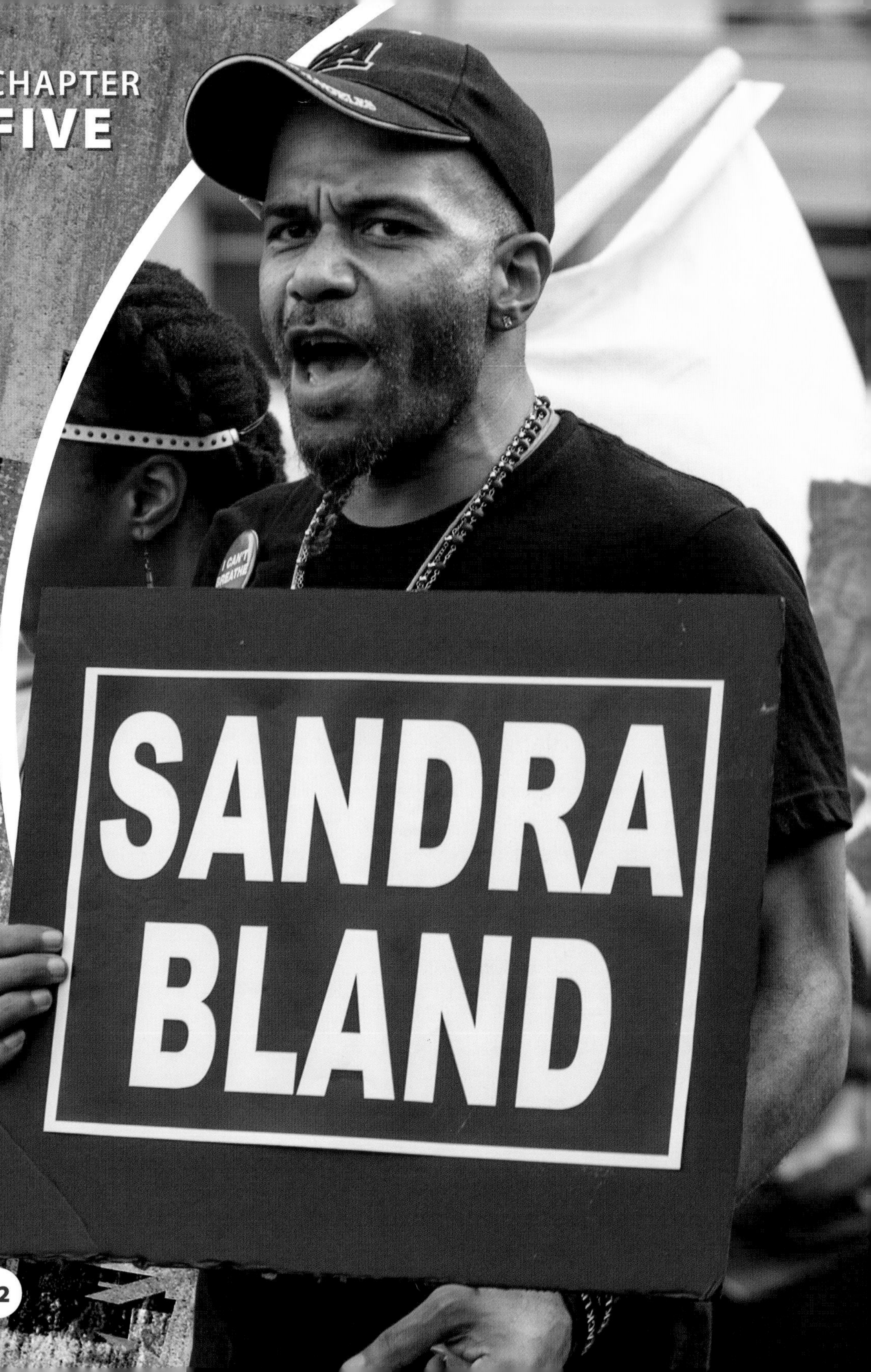

MOVING FORWARD

I n 2015 a new series of police-related deaths rocked the nation. Renewed protests broke out locally and nationally after many of the deaths. Then, in July, Sandra Bland died while in police custody in Texas. The 28-year-old's death was followed by the deaths of several other black women. Their deaths called attention to police treatment of black women.

NEW YEAR, NEW VIOLENCE

The Black Lives Matter Movement seemed to fade in early 2016. But on July 5, 37-year-old black man Alton Sterling was arrested

People protested Bland's death in cities across the nation, including New York City.

PULLING DOWN A SYMBOL

In June 2015, a white gunman entered Emanuel African Methodist Episcopal Church in Charleston, South Carolina. He shot and killed nine African Americans. The shooter wanted to spark a race war. In addition to mourning the killings, Black Lives Matter protested the flying of the Confederate flag over the South Carolina State House. Many saw the flag as a symbol of slavery and racism. Activist Bree Newsome pulled the flag down. She was arrested. But days later, South Carolina removed the Confederate flag from the State House grounds. Activists said the next step was to end the racist views the flag symbolized.

in Baton Rouge, Louisiana. Officers tackled him. They shot him while he was still pinned. The next night, an officer shot 32-year-old Philando Castile near Saint Paul, Minnesota. Castile's girlfriend broadcast the aftermath of the shooting live on Facebook. Sterling's and Castile's deaths set off protests across the country.

One of the cities that held protests was Dallas, Texas. Officers there cooperated with protesters. They roped off areas for demonstrations. Some even posed for photos with protesters. During the protests, a black gunman opened fire. Five officers were killed. The next week, a gunman in Baton Rouge killed three officers. In both cases, the officers were targeted in revenge for police killings of black men. In 2017 the officer who shot Castile was ruled not guilty on all charges.

FORMAL DEMANDS

The Black Lives Matter movement condemned the killings of police officers. But some people blamed the movement for leading people to take violent

STUDENT PROTEST

Black students at the University of Missouri had long complained about their treatment on campus. Many said they faced racial slurs and mistreatment. In 2015 student activists demanded that the college's president step down. They held a camp-in on campus. Student Jonathan Butler went on a hunger strike. The school's football team threatened not to play. The protest was successful. Within a week, the school's president stepped down.

2016 POLICE
KILLINGS

In 2016, police officers in the United States killed 1,093 people. Twenty-four percent of those killed were black. Yet just 13.3 percent of the US population is black. The map below shows where officer-involved deaths happened more and less frequently. What do you notice about the different regions? Why do you think some states have more officer-involved deaths than others?

MORE THAN 20 OFFICER-INVOLVED DEATHS

16–20 OFFICER-INVOLVED DEATHS

11–15 OFFICER-INVOLVED DEATHS

6–10 OFFICER-INVOLVED DEATHS

5 OR FEWER OFFICER-INVOLVED DEATHS

action against officers. Others criticized it for a lack of leadership. Over time the movement had come to include hundreds of organizations. Many critics felt that the presence of so many organizations left the movement leaderless. They wanted to see a single strong leader, like Martin Luther King Jr., emerge. But many within the movement rejected this idea. They felt Black Lives Matter should include many leaders and many groups. Each group could focus on the change it saw as most urgent.

Many critics also said the movement lacked direction. Activists were accused of not having specific goals. But on August 1, 2016, leaders from more than 50 black organizations issued the Vision for Black Lives. The vision laid out several demands. Among them was an end to police violence. Other demands included changes in education. The vision called for free college education for students. It also sought a guaranteed minimum income for all Americans.

CONTINUED WORK

The Vision for Black Lives was released during the 2016 presidential campaign. Throughout the campaign, demonstrators disrupted rallies held by candidates. In at least one case, demonstrators jumped onto the stage and took over the microphone. At rallies for Republican candidate Donald Trump, protesters and Trump supporters sometimes became involved in physical fights.

Democratic candidate Hillary Clinton received support from a group known as the Mothers of the Movement. The group was made up of mothers whose children had been killed in police or racially motivated violence. Clinton invited the mothers to speak at the Democratic National Convention. Their message helped rally many black voters. But some people felt Clinton was taking advantage of the mothers. Others said her campaign did not focus enough on violence against police officers. Clinton lost the election to Trump.

Sandra Bland's mother, Geneva Reed-Veal, is a member of Mothers of the Movement.

President Trump took office in January 2017. Many worried that the new president would allow increased police violence. Many Black Lives Matter organizers changed tactics. They switched from holding large-scale protests to changing local policies. Many felt local actions were more likely to result in positive changes than national efforts.

In its short history, the Black Lives Matter movement has had many successes. More than 85 new state and federal laws addressing police violence have been passed. Black Lives Matter chapters have been established across the United States and overseas. The Justice Department has investigated police departments in several major cities.

Yet much work remains. That work may be done in different ways by different groups. It may focus on different demands. But in the end, the goal of the Black Lives Matter movement is one the United States has struggled with from the beginning: racial equality.

STRAIGHT TO THE
SOURCE

President Obama gave a speech after the killing of five white Dallas police officers:

> *Race relations have improved dramatically in my lifetime. . . . But, America, we know that bias remains. . . . When study after study shows that whites and people of color experience the criminal justice system differently, so that if you're black you're more likely to be pulled over or searched or arrested, more likely to get longer sentences, more likely to get the death penalty for the same crime . . . when all this takes place more than 50 years after the passage of the Civil Rights Act, we cannot simply turn away and dismiss those in peaceful protest as troublemakers or paranoid.*

Source: Barack Obama. "Remarks by the President at Memorial Service for Fallen Dallas Police Officers." *White House*. White House, July 12, 2016. Web. Accessed July 13, 2017.

Point of View

Compare this passage to the one by Tef Poe in Chapter One. Think about the two writers' points of view. Write a short essay that answers these questions: What is the point of view of each author? How are they similar and why? How are they different and why?

FAST FACTS

- The Black Lives Matter movement was formed in response to police shootings of black men. It seeks to end police violence and racial inequalities.

- Key players include Alicia Garza, Patrisse Cullors, Opal Tometi, and DeRay Mckesson.

- Protests against police violence have been held in cities across the United States.

- Black Lives Matter chapters have been established in cities across the United States and abroad. Hundreds of other black activist organizations have also been formed.

- More than 85 state and federal laws addressing police violence have been passed. The US Justice Department has investigated police departments in many cities.

- Protest strategies include die-ins, rallies, and informational booths.

- The Vision for Black Lives laid out the changes the movement wanted to see for black people.

IMPORTANT
DATES

1992
Riots break out in Los Angeles, California, in April after officers accused of beating Rodney King are ruled not guilty.

2013
On July 13, George Zimmerman is acquitted of murdering Trayvon Martin, sparking the creation of the #BlackLivesMatter hashtag.

2014
On August 9, Michael Brown is shot and killed by officer Darren Wilson in Ferguson, Missouri, sparking protests including the Ferguson October protests on October 13. On November 22, 12-year-old Tamir Rice is shot by Cleveland, Ohio, officers. Officials announce two days later that Wilson won't be charged with a crime in Brown's death.

2016
On July 5, an officer shoots Alton Sterling while Sterling is still pinned. The next day, an officer shoots Philando Castile near Saint Paul, Minnesota. His girlfriend streams the aftermath on social media. On August 1, leaders from more than 50 black organizations issue the Vision for Black Lives.

STOP AND
THINK

Tell the Tale

Chapter Three tells how the #BlackLivesMatter hashtag started. Imagine an event has inspired you to create your own hashtag. Write 200 words about the event. What made you want to create a hashtag about it? What hashtag would you use?

Surprise Me

Chapter Two discusses the history of race relations in the United States. After reading this book, what two or three facts about this history did you find most surprising? Write a few sentences about each fact. Why did you find each fact surprising?

Dig Deeper

After reading this book, what questions do you still have about Black Lives Matter? With an adult's help, find a few reliable sources that can help answer your questions. Write a paragraph about what you learned.

GLOSSARY

acquit
for a jury to release someone from the legal charges brought against him or her

civil disobedience
nonviolent refusal to obey laws in order to bring about change

clergy
leaders of religious groups

discrimination
the act of treating someone differently for traits such as race

federal
relating to the central government of a nation

lynch
to kill by hanging, usually carried out by a mob

pepper spray
a spray that causes temporary blindness and pain to the nose, throat, and skin

segregation
a policy of separating people by race

sit-in
an act of protest that involves sitting in seats or on the ground and refusing to leave

tear gas
a substance that is released into the air and causes the eyes to fill with tears, making it difficult to see

ONLINE
RESOURCES

To learn more about Black Lives Matter, visit our free resource websites below.

Visit **abdocorelibrary.com** for free Common Core resources for teachers and students, including vetted activities, multimedia, and booklinks, for deeper subject comprehension.

Visit **abdobooklinks.com** for free additional online weblinks for further learning. These links are routinely monitored and updated to provide the most current information available.

LEARN
MORE

Harris, Duchess. *Civil Rights Sit-Ins*. Minneapolis, MN: Abdo Publishing, 2018.

Uhl, Xina M. *The Passing of the Civil Rights Act of 1964*. Minneapolis, MN: Abdo Publishing, 2016.

ABOUT THE AUTHOR

Duchess Harris, JD, PhD
Professor Harris is the chair of the American Studies Department at Macalester College. The author and coauthor of four books (*Hidden Human Computers: The Black Women of NASA* and *Black Lives Matter* with Sue Bradford Edwards, *Racially Writing the Republic: Racists, Race Rebels, and Transformations of American Identity* with Bruce Baum, and *Black Feminist Politics from Kennedy to Clinton/Obama*), she has been an associate editor for *Litigation News*, the American Bar Association Section's quarterly flagship publication, and was the first editor-in-chief of *Law Raza Journal*, an interactive online race and the law journal for William Mitchell College of Law.

She has earned a PhD in American Studies from the University of Minnesota and a Juris Doctorate from William Mitchell College of Law.

INDEX